EMBRACE

EMBRACE IT! Don't erase it!

By:
Yvette Urquhart

DEDICATION

For all of the amazing people that I have been so blessed to cross paths with on life's journey, this book is dedicated to each of you. The people that I met while waiting for the bus, train, or plane; the ones I chatted with while waiting in line at the grocery store; the lovely women I enjoy holding conversation with at the beauty salon; the thousands of people I have worshiped with on Sunday morning; the millions of people I have passed by on the street, strolled past in the mall; the other mothers and fathers that I have met in the stands at sporting events as we cheered our children on; the wise and spunky elderly mothers at the senior citizens centers.

To all the children I was given the opportunity to be a part of their lives through substitute teaching, volunteering, and children's ministry; my parents, family, friends; to every woman, man, boy, or girl I have ever met; I say thank you! I thank you because you have inspired, encouraged, and empowered me to do what I do.

This book is a manifestation of conversations, prayers, concerns, hurts, hopes, and dreams that you have expressed to me directly or indirectly, which God has inspired me to compile to share with the world. It is my desire that this book will touch, influence, motivate, stimulate, transform, and bless the reader's life in such a way that they will EMBRACE life and live life like never before.

TABLE OF CONTENT

INTRODUCTION

EMBRACE

1. To submit to, accept completely.
2. Receive, seize, make use of.
3. To avail oneself to.
4. Receive willingly and/or enthusiastically.
5. Embody, take in.
6. Accept (opportunity, challenge, etc.) willingly or eagerly.

ERASE

1. Remove all traces of (a thought, feeling or memory); to destroy or remove something completely.
2. No longer remember an emotion.
3. Remove any sign of; obliterate, as from the mind.
4. To get rid of an unpleasant memory, feeling or thought.

EMBRACE IT! Don't erase it!

CHAPTER 1

INTRODUCTION
EMBRACE IT!

Don't erase it! It Happened

I am sure that all of us have experienced some things in life that we wish would have never happened, wish we would have never said, wish we could forget or turn back the hands of time or do it differently. We have done things we regret, made bad decisions we wish we could change, and spoke harsh words that we wish we could take back. We can't change what has been done. We can't retrieve words once they have been spoken. If we had a gigantic eraser, knew magic, or had the power to make things disappear, we would. However, the reality of it all is, what's done is done, period. We can try to make it better, regret what we did, ask for forgiveness, kiss and make-up, but we can't erase it.

Nothing we say or do can change the fact that it happened. We can ignore it, try to forget about it, and overlook it, but it happened. It may be hard to face, hard to admit, and painful to accept, but it happened. We can deny it, wish it would never have happened, hope that we will wake up and it will be just one horrible nightmare, but it happened. You may want to change, delete, edit, or erase it, but it happened. You can fuss, cry, curse, be mad, angry, and throw a fit, but once you come off the emotional roller coaster, you still have to face the fact that it happened.

Life happens, and there are just some things we can't change. We must accept the good, the bad, the ugly, the painful, the chaos, the tragedy, the drama, the trauma; we want to make it go away, disappear, but it happened. We need to learn to accept the things we can't change and pray that God will give us the wisdom to accept what has happened, heal from it, learn from it, grow from it, and move forward.

"Brethren, I count not myself to have apprehended: but this one thing I do, forgetting those things which are behind, and reaching forth unto those things which are before, I press toward the mark for the prize of the high calling of God in Christ Jesus" (Philippians 3:13–14). It happened, so embrace it; don't try to erase it but celebrate because, out of all the things that you have encountered or experienced in your life, the fact that you are still here is proof that you have endured it all! It happened; accept it, receive it, EMBRACE it!

CHAPTER 2

EMBRACE WHO YOU ARE

No Apologies Necessary

You owe no man/woman an explanation for who you are! God created you exactly the way He wanted you to be. He did not ask for, nor did He need, anyone's opinion or approval concerning you. God did not need anyone to co-sign, nor did He need anyone to inspect, His work. When God created you, He patted himself on the back and said, "Now, that is very good! Man with his critical self may beg to differ." People are always finding fault in others.

There are those who feel we must measure up to their expectations. They think they are the authority over how we should act, look, dress, talk, conduct ourselves, etc. We don't need to make any apologies because we don't live up to their expectations of us. We don't have to answer to or please anyone but God. Don't try to conform to please people. If they can't accept you exactly as you are, then you don't need them in your life. Don't try to explain, make excuses, or validate why you are the way you are. Stop apologizing to people for being you! You are rare, unique, and one of a kind. If there is anything about you that needs fixing, God will do the transforming. He doesn't need man's help with anything regarding you. You are you, and that's that! No apologies necessary. Go ahead and fully embrace the you that God created you to be.

Be Who You Are

Be Who You Are
Everyone else is taken.
Don't try to be someone else.
Be the real you and not an imitation.

Do it how you do it. And do what you do.
Don't try to be me. And I shouldn't try to be you.

God made us all different.
There is nothing wrong with being yourself.
You are one of a kind. There is no rule that says you
have to be like everyone else.

God made you special with your own unique
characteristics and talent too. So, who cares what other
people say or think?
You just keep on being you.

Take off the mask of being someone else.
To thine own self be true.
Don't fake it; don't be ashamed of it; don't deny it.
Just be 100% wonderful you!

CHAPTER 3

EMBRACE THE MESS

God Is the Janitor of Your Soul

Have you ever felt as if your life is a complete mess, just a total shipwreck? Have you ever felt broken, shattered into a million pieces and beyond repair? Have you ever felt like nothing seems to work out for you? Your home got foreclosed on; your car was repossessed; you lost your job, custody of your kids; you had been strung out on drugs; you are an alcoholic; you have been molested, arrested, abused. Every time you turn around, there just seems to be one thing after the other. You feel you just can't catch a break.

You try your hardest and still can't get it together. While you are going through your trouble, your trials, your dark place, the devil comes along to try to keep you discouraged. He reminds you of how much of a mess you are. He tries to convince you that you are indeed hopeless, helpless, and a twisted-up mess that can't be untangled. Don't believe the lies the devil keeps whispering in your ear. You see, the devil knows that

6

behind all that mess is a blessed individual. He got kicked out of the garden of Eden for being messy, and now he wants you to miss out on all the great things God has planned for your life.

Satan knows that there is no hope for him, and he wants to trick you into thinking that there is no hope for you.

I am so glad that we have hope and a future. No matter what mess our life story may hold, through the grace and power of God, we can be washed clean. Embrace the mess because God will bless in spite of our mess.

He Saw The Best In Me

He saw the best in me.
He saw what the natural eye cannot see.
He saw me for who I am
while others were caught up in how
messed-up I used to be.

He saw the best of me.
He saw beyond all the drugs, alcohol, sex,
and lies that had contaminated me.
He looked beyond all my faults,
and He saw His love was all I needed.

He saw the best in me.
While others mocked and laughed as
they saw me bound by the enemy, He saw
the potential that lies within.
He saw me for the person He is going to mold me to be.

He saw the best in me.
He saw me even before I was conceived.
He saw the blessed in me.
You only saw my yesterday and today,
but He saw my destiny.

CHAPTER 4

EMBRACE YOUR UNIQUENESS

Not Strange; Just Different

Be weird, a nerd, different, an outsider, awkward, a misfit; it's OK. God did not create you to blend in but to stand out. There is no law that says you have to be like anyone else.

Who says the next person is better than you? "For God shows no partiality [no arbitrary favoritism; with Him, one person is not more important than another]" (Romans 2:11, AMP). It's perfectly all right for you to march to a different beat, dance to a different tune, and blaze a new path. Stop worrying about whether or not people like you.

You don't have to do what everybody else does. You don't have to do it like they do it. Just because you are not part of the click, a member of the club, or belong to the in-crowd doesn't make you strange.

Do your own thing. Do it your way. Do it how you do it and do what you do. There is nothing special or interesting about being the same as everyone else. It takes courage and guts to be you. People don't understand you, but that is quite all right, as long as they respect your peculiarity and uniqueness. Don't change who you are; embrace it!

I Want To Be Like Me

I want to be like me.
I want to be the me God created me to be.
I don't have to be like everyone else.
God loves me for me.

I may not have a college degree.
I may not speak very eloquently.
Yet when I open up my mouth to speak or pray,
God hears every word I say.

I may not be in on the latest style of dress.
When you look at me, you may not be impressed.
But I am confident in what God says about me.
He said I am made fearfully and wonderfully.

Your opinion of me is really not my concern.
Being comfortable with who I am is something I have
long learned.

God is my designer, and He created me just the way He
wanted me to be.

Therefore, I love, embrace, and enjoy
being different, unique ole me!

CHAPTER 5:

EMBRACE YOUR IMPERFECTIONS

Perfectly Flawed

You may not be perfect, but you sure are precious. You may not feel precious. You may feel as if you have a million things wrong with you. You reflect on so many things about yourself that you are dissatisfied with and wish you could change.

You may compare yourself to others, desiring to be like them to have their skin, height, hair, legs, weight, and perhaps their life. You look at others, and it appears that they are perfect and have it all together.

You may feel insecure because of a disability, a skin disorder, a speech impediment, or other challenges that cause you to think you are imperfect and flawed. There is absolutely nothing wrong with you.

You are perfect just the way you are. Those things that you see as imperfections are actually what make you so special. Please know that you are perfectly imperfect and fabulously flawed.

11

God loves you unconditionally, flaws and all. "And he said unto me, My grace is sufficient for thee: for my strength is made perfect in weakness. Most gladly therefore will I rather glory in my infirmities, that the power of Christ may rest upon them" (2 Corinthians 12:9).

MIRROR, MIRROR

Today, I am setting myself free.
I am no longer allowing the chains of negativity
and low self-esteem bind me.

I allowed the enemy to bamboozle
and trick me for far too long,
making me think I wasn't good enough, smart enough,
tall enough, talented enough, and valuable enough;
making me feel as if everything about
me was oh so wrong.

At times I felt so insignificant.
I struggled with insecurity.
I didn't quite understand who I was.
So I searched the scriptures to see
what God says about me.
That's when I found out who I really am
and discovered my true identity.

Mirror, mirror, I am so excited, you see.
Because I found out all of the wonderful
things God says about me.

God says I am fearfully and wonderfully made.
Therefore, I am not worried about what
other people think or say.

I have been accepted.
So, I don't have to fit in your click, join your sorority, or
become a member of a certain club.

I've been restored, redeemed, forgiven, purchased by the
shedding of Jesus' blood.

I am His child; I love God, and He loves me.
I am chosen, God's special possession, a queen;
I'm royalty.
I love me some me and the amazing person God has
created me to be.

He created me special by design.
I am rare, unique, one of a kind.
I am enough; I'm worthy
absolutely, totally, and completely.

I am done. I am over with trying to be like and please
everyone else.

There's only one me, and God wants me to be myself.
Mirror, mirror on the wall,
I am definitely the fairest of them all.
I am just as fabulous as I can be.
I am learning to love, celebrate, embrace,
and enjoy being me.

All of my imperfections;
all of my flaws;
God loves me unconditionally in spite of them all.

CHAPTER 6

EMBRACE THE REAL YOU

Be Who You Are

Keep it 100. Keep it real. You don't have to fake it, and you need to cut out the phony. You don't have to imitate or pretend to be who you are NOT. You don't have to hide behind a mask or disguise your identity. Cut out the drama and stop putting on a show, trying to impress people. You're so busy trying to be like everyone else that you have forgotten who you are. Why would you want to be a carbon copy when you were created to be an original?

God doesn't make factory seconds! You won't have to try so hard or fail so miserably if you just be yourself. Why are you trying so hard to be someone else when you are the real deal yourself? Appreciate yourself. Celebrate yourself. You are intelligent, creative, talented, loving, awesome, amazing, giving, strong, an overcomer, more than a conqueror and the list goes on regarding just how incredible you are. Be yourself and embrace the real you.

Allow your true self to shine through. People may be able to beat you at a lot of things, but can't nobody beat you at being you. You are the expert, the genius, the guru at being you. Enjoy being you because there is no one else in the universe like you. If you don't be you, then who will?

Love Yourself
Self-love Pledge

I promise to love and accept myself unconditionally.
I will see myself not as man but how God sees me.
I embrace my imperfections, flaws, faults, and shortcomings.
I accept that I am a work in progress and that God's grace is sufficient.

I will not be ashamed of who I am or what I have done because Jesus paid the price on Calvary, and I have been forgiven.
I accept, and I am OK with the fact that I am not perfect, but I am precious, priceless, and full of purpose.

I pledge to be so caught up in being the me that God created me to be that I have absolutely no time to wish I was or pretend to be someone else.
I am the original, the master copy!

Why would I want to be anyone else when God made me so awesome, amazing, fierce, fabulous, talented, creative, anointed, loving, irresistible, and favored?

I promise to love me, accept me, be satisfied with me, respect me, forgive me, and to never underestimate my self-worth and value.

I am learning to be content with who I am and whose I am.
I finally feel relaxed and at home in my own skin.
Loving and truly being me has never felt so good!

CHAPTER 7

EMBRACE IT; DON'T ERASE IT

Face It

Our lives are a melting pot of experiences love and hate, joy and pain, happiness and grief, trials and triumphs, tragedies and celebrations, life and death, wins and losses, marriage and divorce, addictions and recovery, defeat and victory, and the list goes on. It's easy to face the good that life brings our way, but when life is ugly, painful, and unfair, we would rather those moments pass us by. However, life is not quite that simple. Life can be rather complicated at times. When we accept the hand we have been dealt and face it, then we can begin to get a handle on it and move forward.

Once we have come to grips that it happened, then we can face it. Some things are so painful, dramatic, tragic, and traumatic that we find it hard and almost impossible to gather the strength to face it. We wish that it would just go away, but it happened, and it is imperative that we face it so we can move past it. I realize that facing it is much easier said than done. Some things take time, and we have to process what has happened before we are able to face it. We don't have to face life's storms alone. "Cast your burdens on the Lord and he shall sustain you" (Psalms 55:22). God will gladly help us and give us the courage and strength that we need to face each day.

I want to give you some scriptures to read to remind you that when you are going through the ups and downs of life, there is hope, help, and healing for you. You can find encouragement and comfort in God's Word.

"So I am well pleased with weaknesses, with insults, with distresses, with persecutions, and with difficulties, for the sake of Christ; for when I am weak [in human strength], then I am strong [truly able, truly powerful, truly drawing from God's strength]."

–2 Corinthians 12:10 AMP

"My flesh and my heart may fail, But God is the rock and strength of my heart and my portion forever."

–Psalms 73:26

"He giveth power to the faint; and to them that have no might he increaseth strength."

–Isaiah 40:29

"Finally, my brethren, be strong in the Lord, and in the power of his might."

–Ephesians 6:10

19

"And let us not be weary in well doing: for in due season we shall reap, if we faint not."

–Galatians 6:9

CHAPTER 8

EMBRACE LOVING YOU

Fall in Love with You

How can you expect someone else to love you when you don't even love you? You may not love everything about yourself, but you shouldn't let that stop you from loving you. It's essential for your personal evolution that you learn to love yourself. We all have some things about us we don't particularly care for or that we wish we could change. You don't have to be perfect to love yourself. You don't have to have it all together in order to love yourself. You need to fall in love with the man/woman in the mirror.

You are spending too much time comparing yourself to and trying to measure up to others when there is absolutely nothing wrong with you! Overcome those nasty, self-negative thoughts. Stop focusing on all the things you dislike about yourself and learn to unconditionally love you. Love your curves, your thick lips, your long hair, your short hair, your curly hair, your kinky hair, your big nose, your crooked nose, your big eyes, your little squinty eyes, your height, your pimples, your freckles, your wrinkles, your stretch marks, your chicken legs, your large calves, your big feet, your small figure, your full figure, etc.

All of these things are a part of who you are; therefore, learn to love and embrace everything about you. Appreciate yourself, respect yourself, and recognize the amazing person you are. You love others, and others love you. Now, how about loving yourself? Whitney Houston said it best, "Learning to love yourself is the greatest love of all."

Positive Affirmations
of Love for Yourself

I love me some me.
I love myself deeply and completely.
I am loved.
I am worthy of love.
I love the me God created me to be.
I love myself unconditionally.
I love myself in spite of all my flaws and imperfections.
I love myself just the way I am.
I will forgive myself when I make a mistake.
I am beautiful.
I am enough.
I know my worth.
I am whole.
I am fearfully and wonderfully made.
I am fierce, fabulous, and favored.

I matter.

I deserve to be happy and loved.

I am a blessing.

I am confident in who I am and whose I am.

I am kind, generous, and loving.

I am intelligent, capable, and competent.

I was created with divine intention.

I am an amazingly awesome individual.

I appreciate and respect myself.

I love absolutely everything about me.

CHAPTER 9

EMBRACE YOUR GREATNESS

Believe in You

You are absolutely awesome. There is greatness in you! You are talented, creative, and can accomplish anything you set your mind to do. Believe it, and you can achieve it. Everything you need to reach your goals and manifest your dreams lies within you. Perhaps you don't have the finances, the education; you were raised on the wrong side of the tracks or don't look the part. Maybe someone lied to you and told you that you can't do it, you don't have what it takes. They may have told you that your past will hold you back. Lies! All lies! Don't allow all the can'ts to prevent you from believing that you can.

You may have to work hard; there may be roadblocks and setbacks and even some failure along the way, but don't you dare stop believing in you. You definitely have what it takes. Never stop believing in yourself. If no one else believes in you, then encourage yourself. Be your own cheerleader! You need to turn a deaf ear to the negative chatter of others who are trying to stop your progress and discourage you from following your dreams and fulfilling your purpose. Matthew 11:24 reminds us that whatever we ask in prayer and believe that we have received will be ours.

Don't become distracted by what it looks like or feels like. Just know that if you keep grinding, continue following your dream, keep reaching for the stars, tap into all the greatness that lies within you, stay persistent and consistent, never quit, never stop believing in you, then you will be unstoppable! Remember, all things are possible if you only believe.

Encourage Yourself

You can't always wait on the preacher or prophet.
You can't always depend on somebody else.
Sometimes you have to look in the mirror
and just encourage yourself.

Sometimes you need a word.
There may be no one else around.
So, you just have to encourage your own self
when you are discouraged or feeling a little down.

Sometimes you have to speak a word over yourself.
You must know who you are in Christ.
When it feels like your situation is speaking death,
you must open up your mouth and speak life.

You must encourage yourself
when the devil tries to crowd your mind
with negative things.
You must speak that you are the head and not the tail.
You are royalty, a child of the King!

Encourage yourself.
Always carry in your heart an encouraging word or song.
Speak a positive word over yourself.
Remember that life and death are in the power
of your own tongue.

Speak over yourself.
Don't allow trials, tribulations, stumbling blocks,
or storms contaminate the words that depart from
your lips.
Tap into the power of God that lies within you.
Now is not the time to trip.

Encourage yourself; minister to yourself.
That is all you need to do.
You don't have to rely on the words of others.
You have the power to speak over yourself and
allow your own words to see you through.

Speak to yourself!
Believe in yourself!
Minister to yourself!
Encourage yourself!

CHAPTER 10

EMBRACE YOUR BIRTHRIGHT

You Are Royalty

You are not just anybody. You are more than the name on your birth certificate. You are more than where you were born and who your parents are. You are more than the schools you attended, the education you received, the positions you have held, and so much more than even your greatest accomplishments.

You are royalty, a child of the King. Don't you ever allow anyone, anything, or any circumstance cause you to feel as if you don't measure up to others. We are sons and daughters of God; heirs to the kingdom. We belong to an aristocratic dynasty. The enemy doesn't want us to know who we really are. We may live in a world where beauty, money, fame, education, and status are coveted, but all of these things are temporal.

If we don't accomplish or achieve all of these things during our lifetime, that does not negate the fact that we are royalty. Our royalty is not based on the standards and acceptance of this world. We are royalty because our brother, Jesus, is the King of Kings. We are the sons and daughters of God. What higher position can we occupy than to be called the sons and daughters of our Father who is the King of all Nations!

You may not feel like royalty or look like royalty, but there is a king/queen inside of you. "But ye are a chosen generation, a royal priesthood, an holy nation, a peculiar people" (1Peter 2:9). My friend, you need to understand who you truly are! Own it. Walk in it. Live up to it. You are royalty, so go ahead and embrace it!

You Are Royalty

I am an element of royalty.
I belong to an aristocratic dynasty.
I am clothed with strength and dignity.
There is a queen, a king, in me.
There's so much more to me than the natural eye can see.
I am adopted, chosen, accepted; I am royalty.
God has hidden so much greatness inside of me;
He has given me hope, a future, a destiny.
I am royalty.
I am confident in my identity.
I am royalty.
Not because of who I am but because of God in me!

CHAPTER 11

EMBRACE YOUR SCARS

Proof that You Survived

A lot of us have scars. Some scars are nasty, ugly, and the center of attention. Some scars, we can cover up, and other scars are hidden from the natural eye. Some scars are physical, while others are emotional wounds. We don't like to talk about our scars. We don't want others to notice our scars and will go to great lengths to conceal them. Some of us are ashamed or embarrassed by our scars.

They can be unattractive, painful, and can make us feel imperfect and uncomfortable, yet they don't define us. Satan wants to keep you so distracted by and consumed with the scar until it is magnified, and all you can see and are reminded of constantly is that scar. I encourage you to change your mindset and stop looking at your scars as scars but think of them as battle wounds.

The beauty in the scar is that it signifies that you were wounded, but you won. It serves as a reminder that what you went through did not kill you. In the future, when you see or think about your scar, allow it to fill your heart with joy and gladness, celebrating the fact that you are a warrior. You were hurt, wounded, scared, and injured, but you endured, persevered, and survived! After all, even Jesus had scars. There were physical scars, as His hands and feet were nailed to the cross, and He was pierced in His side. Then there were deeper emotional scars of having people, and ultimately His own father, turn their backs on Him as He endured the agony of the cross. Jesus' scars symbolize the pain, but even more so, they represent His unconditional mercy and love toward us.

I recently listened to a song, "Flawless," by Mercy Me, and the message so clearly speaks to us about embracing our scars:

No matter the bumps, No matter the bruises,
No matter the scars, still the truth is,
The cross has made, the cross has made you flawless.
No matter the hurt, or how deep the wound is,
No matter the pain, still the truth is,
The cross has made, the cross has made you flawless.

Embrace your scars and allow them to serve as a memorial of the pain you have endured and the battles you have won!

I'M A SURVIVOR

I have been oppressed,
distressed,
depressed,
and a complete mess, but I survived.
I have been put down,
thrown down,
and held down, but I survived.
I have been mistreated,
depleted,
cheated,
and almost defeated, but I survived.
I have been choked,
broke,
looked at as a joke,
and put down by church folk, but I survived.
I have been knocked upside the head,
beat up and dragged,
thrown around like a dirty rag,
and left for dead, yet I survived.
I have been molested,
arrested,
injected,
and infected, yet I survived.
I have been ashamed,
defamed,
called everything but my name,
and almost driven totally insane, yet I survived.
I survived;

I'm still alive.
God was on my side;
He said I shall live and not die!
I survived.
I survived.
I survived.
I survived because of the blood He shed.
I survived because of the crown of thorns placed upon
His head.
I survived because He died.
I survived because He is still alive.
I survived because He had a plan for me.
God said I shall not be destroyed by the hand of the
enemy.
But from the chains of the past, I would be set free.
Now, all my pain and suffering has turned into victory.
I survived.
You survived.
We survived.

CHAPTER 12

EMBRACE YOUR FREEDOM

No Longer Bound

The devil desires to keep you bound, shackled, chained; held hostage to your past, your failures, your fears, your pain, and all those things that make you ashamed and prevent you from being free. Satan wants to see you living in fear, angry, depressed, disoriented, confused, mourning, grieving, desperate, weak, stuck, disengaged, brainwashed, lifeless, hopeless, crippled, irritated, weak, wounded, and weighed down with the cares of life. Satan is afraid that if and when you become aware that

God wants you to be free, he will no longer have authority, control, or power over your life. Satan wants to keep you tangled and tied up because he knows that if the Son sets you free, you will be free indeed (John 8:36, NIV). Satan is well aware that when God sets you free, He will loose the shackles, destroy yokes, break chains, and loose strongholds. Satan is concerned because he knows that when you realize that you are free, alive indeed, an overcomer, survivor, victorious, a champion, chosen, holy, blessed, and highly favored, you will be UNSTOPPABLE!

When you are free, the enemy will neither be able to intimidate you with his schemes nor trick you with his foolery. He knows that once you recognize who you are in Christ, hell is going to be in trouble! Hell is going to be in for a fight because you are no longer bound but now aware, alert, and equipped to stand firm against him. Keep your eyes in the Word, your knees bent, your hands lifted, and your mind stayed on Jesus. You have been released. Don't look back; don't go back but embrace your freedom! Christ has set us free to live a free life. So, take your stand! Never again let anyone put a harness of slavery on you (Galatians 5:1, MSG).

BREAKING THE CHAINS

I'm breaking the chain off my mind.
I'm breaking the chains off my heart.
I'm no longer bound.
I'm free to make a brand new start.

I'm breaking the chains off my eyes.
Now I can clearly see
all of the wonderful blessings
God has in store for me.

I'm breaking the chains off my hands
so I can give Him a wave.
I'm breaking the chains off my tongue
so I can give God the highest praise.

I'm breaking the chains off my legs.
I'm breaking the chains off my feet.
I'm tired of being bound.
Today, I am setting myself free!

I'm breaking the chains of all the hurt.
I'm breaking the chains of all the pain.
I'm breaking the chains of all the thoughts
that tried to drive me insane.

I'm breaking the chains that hold me down.
I'm breaking the chains that kept me bound.
I am shaking myself loose.
Nothing can stop me now.

I am stepping out with strength.
I am stepping out with power.
I'm taking my life back.
Yes, this is my hour!
I'm breaking the chains; I'm free!

CHAPTER 13

EMBRACE YOUR PAST

It's History

It happened. It's over and done. You want to forget about it, and you have some regrets. However, the enemy feels the need to constantly remind you of all of your shortcomings, inadequacies, failures, and mistakes. He wants you to hold on to those things that you cannot change. The enemy wants to remind you of who you were and all the wrong that you used to do.

He wants us to relive over and over all the sins we have committed and poor choices we have made. He derives great pleasure from seeing us burdened down with the shame and guilt from our past. He enjoys seeing us stuck, trapped, and looking in the rearview mirror. He carefully and strategically scans through the history of our lives and replays those things that will bombard us with embarrassment and disgrace. He specializes in digging up the dirt and finding those things that cut sharp and wound deeply.

We can't stay stuck in our past. We must serve notice on the devil. It's time to give him an eviction notice. Look him dead in the face; stand toe to toe with him and let him know that he will no longer hold us hostage to our past. We have hope and a future. Tell him that he can no longer threaten you or assault you about your past. "Forget the former things; do not dwell on the past. See, I am doing a new thing" (Isaiah 43:18–19). You no longer have to continuously live in shame and regret because of God's grace and mercy; you can walk in confidence and assurance.

Don't waste another day grieving over your past. Learn from it; heal from it; embrace it; let it go and move on.

BAG LADY

Bag lady, it is time for you to dump those bags.
They are holding you up and causing you to drag.
It is time for you to move ahead.
Yet you continue going around and around in circles.

You should be further along in your journey in life.
But past relationships and resentments have caused you
to lose focus and lose sight.
Girl, it's time you snap out of this hypnosis state you're
in.
Life is a game, and you must play to win.

It is past time for you to move on.
You have already wasted too much precious time.
Holding on to all this baggage
is causing you to be left behind.

Sister, please dump those bags
so you can ease on down the road.
You cannot move forward
if you continue carrying such a heavy load.

All of the hurt and pain you feel deep within;
just let it go throw it to the wind.
Life has too much to offer; the future has
too much in store.
You must not allow the past to continue to haunt you
anymore.

I've been where you are. I know how you feel.
I had to nourish my old wounds and allow them to heal.
Once I let go of those things that for
so long hindered me,
I felt like a caged eagle that had finally been set free.

Let go of all that baggage, my sister.
You can do it if you try.
You have been grounded far too long.
It's time you spread your wings and fly.

Carrying all that baggage can be pretty
hard on your back.
Shake off that heavy load.
Pack light
so you can ease on down the road.

CHAPTER 14

EMBRACE YOUR FEARS

Don't Be Afraid

Why are you afraid? What is that thing that scares you? What is it that intimidates you and keeps you paralyzed with fear? Stop worrying about whether or not you can do it, if you are good enough. *Do I have what it takes? Will people like me? What if I fail miserably? What if, what if?* We can come up with a million excuses. We have become experts at over-analyzing, over-thinking, and talking ourselves out of doing what we know God has called us to do.

Well, what if you don't do it? Sometimes you just have to do it afraid. It's not always about you. The gifts, talents, abilities, dreams, passions, and visions God has deposited inside of you are not necessarily for or about you. Someone else's life may be dependent upon you stepping out of fear and taking a leap of faith. A lot of times, we are the vessel God uses to blaze the trail, open the door, and provide opportunities so that others may be blessed because of the assignment He has given us.

Their destiny, their sanity, their survival could be tied to that very thing we fear.

We have an adversary, the devil, who knows all of the greatness God has placed inside of you. The devil wants to magnify your fear and cripple you with anxiety so that he can abort your assignment. The devil is a big bully. He tries to scare us and make us think he is in control. He wants to keep us running scared, but God has not given us the spirit of fear but of power (2 Timothy 1:7). The enemy is actually scared of you.

He is afraid that if you conquer your fears, he will not only have trouble from us but also from all of the other lives that are going to be impacted and empowered when we face our fears. Go ahead; embrace your fears, walking confidently, boldly, and fearlessly down the path God has paved for your life.

Scriptures to Speak and Hear when Faced with Fear

"The LORD is my light and my salvation whom shall I fear? The LORD is the stronghold of my life of whom shall I be afraid?" –Psalm 27:1

"For God has not given us a spirit of fear, but of power and of love and of a sound mind." –2 Timothy 1:7

"So we can confidently say, 'The Lord is my helper; I will not fear; what can man do to me?'" –Hebrews 13:6

"Be strong and courageous. Do not fear or be in dread of them, for it is the Lord your God who goes with you. He will not leave you or forsake you." –Deuteronomy 31:6

"Give all your worries and cares to God, for he cares about you." –1 Peter 5:7

"Peace I leave with you, my peace I give you. I do not give to you as the world gives. Do not let your heart be troubled and do not be afraid." –John 14:27

"'Do not be afraid of them [or their hostile faces], For I am with you [always] to protect you and deliver you,' says the LORD." –Jeremiah 1:8

"Have I not commanded you? Be strong and courageous! Do not be terrified or dismayed (intimidated), for the LORD your God is with you wherever you go."
–Joshua 1:9

"No weapon that is formed against thee shall prosper; and every tongue that shall rise against thee in judgment thou shalt condemn. This is the heritage of the servants of the LORD, and their righteousness is of me, saith the LORD."
–Isaiah 54:17

CHAPTER 15

EMBRACE THE STRUGGLE

It's Part of the Journey

All of your life, you had to fight. It's been one struggle after another. The struggle appears to be endless. You entered this world wrestling to survive because you were born addicted to drugs. Your family was poor, and your parents had to scuffle for everything. You have been struggling, hoping, praying that you would live to see the next moment because of violence and abuse. You have struggled hours, days, months, and years due to molestation, sexual assault, and abuse that has left you damaged and wounded both physically and mentally. The struggle has followed you and refuses to give you a break. You have struggled in your marriage; trouble with children, finances, jobs, health, you name it. The struggle is real. As daunting, painful, and negative as struggle can be, we often stumble across our true strength during the process.

All of us have been in a storm, are currently going through a storm, or will be facing a storm. Struggles, problems, loneliness, death, trials, and tragedy are all a part of life. We are going to have trouble. I don't care how good you are; if you live on this earth a few days, you will face adversity. Man that is born of a woman is of few days and full of trouble. God has already told us that we are going to face trouble. Don't be dismayed and don't get discouraged.

What we don't want to do is to focus on the struggle, giving it the power to cause us to give up, stop, or quit. There is hope, help, relief, and assurance. "I have told you these things so that in me you may have peace. In this world, you will have trouble. But take heart! I have overcome the world" (John 16:33). The struggle did not come to stop you or kill you but to prepare you, position you, and propel you forward. God's will is not that you are weakened to the point of giving up and grow weary during the storm. His desire is to see you grow, gain strength and endurance in the midst of your struggles. Remember, every struggle you've faced in your life has shaped you into the person you are today. Tough times build character and faith. You have a reason to rejoice; you made it; you did it; you endured; you persevered; you survived! Embrace the struggle; it's a vital part of your story.

I'm Still Here

I've weathered the storm.
I made it through the rain.
I've had some heartache.

I have endured some pain.
Yet, in spite of the many things I have encountered
down through the years,
I made it; I'm still here!

I have been talked about.
Lord knows I have been criticized.
I have been overlooked.
Many times I have been pushed aside.
I have been lied on by those I hold so dear,
but that is quite all right because I'm still here!

I have been on the mountaintop.
I've been in the valley low.
I have been through the wilderness,
and I have stood at the crossroads of life, wondering
which way to go.
Even in the midst of all the obstacles, I have had no
need to fear,
for God has been by my side every step of the way. I'm
still here!

I've had friends walk away.
Many times I felt so alone.
Sometimes I felt helpless in a situation,
It appeared as if all hope was gone.
There were even times that I felt as if God was nowhere
near.
He never left me alone; I'm still here!

I have shed many tears.
There were times I stayed awake all night long.
I've felt like giving up a time or two.
I just didn't have the strength to journey on.
But deep down in my spirit, there was determination and
prayer.
By the grace and mercy of God, I'm still here!

There were others who did not make it.
Some were not willing to fight,
but I've come too far to give up now.
I must stand with all my might.
Old Satan thought he had me defeated,
but I just want to make one thing crystal clear—
I am standing on the promises of God; that is why I'm
still here!

CHAPTER 16

EMBRACE YOUR FAILURES

Sometimes You Have to Lose Before You Win

Everyone wants to succeed. We all desire to do our best and be our best. In reality, we must realize that there will be times we will fail. Don't despise failure. Don't beat yourself up or consider yourself less than because of failure. We experience failure in love, relationships, jobs, parenting, finances, and many other areas of our lives. We may fall hard. Failure can be painful and depressing.

As devastating as failure can be, there is still so much more we can learn from failure. We can learn more from failure than all the success in the world can teach us. We learn lessons, gather strength, gain knowledge, and acquire wisdom. If you take time to observe a young toddler, you will notice that they fall many times before they perfect their walking skills. It's in the falling down and getting back up that the toddler learns to stand steady on their feet and walk without fear of always falling. It doesn't matter how many times you fail; as long as you don't give up. Failure is often a critical ingredient on the path to success.

Achieving greatness does not come that easy whatsoever. I am sure that if you were afforded the opportunity to interview some famous people such as Walt Disney, Bill Gates, Oprah Winfrey, Michael Jordan, and many others, you will find that all of them experienced failure at some point in their life, but they didn't stop. Failure is not final, fatal, nor does it mean you are finished or done. Failure will not overtake you. Hard work, courage, persistence, consistency, patience, passion, and sheer determination will turn things around for you. Remember, fighters never quit, and quitters never win. Embrace failure, knowing we can do "ALL" things through Christ who gives us strength (Philippians 4:13).

QUITTERS NEVER WIN

When trouble gets you down,
don't give up and don't give in
because fighters never quit,
and quitters never win.

How can you reach the mountain top
if you are not willing to climb?
How can you obtain life's treasures
if you are not willing to seek so that you might find?

How can you move ahead
if you keep standing in the same place?
How can you win the marathon
if you never enter the race?

How can you achieve
if you never try?
How can you know the answers
if you never ask the reasons why?

How can you accomplish anything
if you always doubt?
How can you succeed
if you never believe things will work out?

How can you win the battle
if you are too scared to fight?
How can you taste how good life can be
if you are not willing to take a bite?

Sometimes life punches you with some serious blows,
and you may feel you have no other alternative
than to give in.
Don't be intimidated; don't give up
because quitters never win.

CHAPTER 17

EMBRACE YOUR ISSUES

Remove the Mask

We all have some issues. Some of us dare not admit, but we do. We have some insecurities, some hidden things, some secrets. Many of us live a life of deception, hiding behind the mask, the make-up, and our designer clothes. We disguise ourselves for public display, thinking we are fooling everyone else when we are only deceiving ourselves. We have issues that we contain behind the confines of our home. We dare not let it slip that we have issues; things we can't deal with, need help with but won't reveal to anyone for fear of being judged. We wear a smile on our face, yet, on the inside, we are hurting, aching, and perhaps even dying because, instead of facing, we are masking our issues.

We wish, hope, and pray that our issues will resolve themselves, magically disappear or if we ignore them, then they will cease to exist. We are still being haunted by trauma from our childhood, an abusive relationship, addictions and other struggles, trials, and tragedies that life has thrown our way. We are depressed, lonely, afraid of being alone, having suicidal thoughts, and engaging in unhealthy behaviors all because we can't cope with our issues.

Please understand that your issue "ain't" going nowhere until you deal with it. Remember, your issue does not define you. Stop trying to ignore it, escape it, bury it, dismiss it, or brush it to the side. The best way to deal with it is to face it. Stop hiding, faking, pretending, masking, and camouflaging it; those are not the answers. No more hiding it, running from it, or ignoring our issues. Don't waste another moment or spend another day being troubled, distressed, tense, uneasy, or worried about your issue(s). No more allowing the issue to control us; we must take control of it. It's time to identify the issue, face it, and get delivered from our issues so that we can find peace, harmony, and joy in our lives. There is an answer, a solution, help, resolution for every issue we face. So, embrace it! "Do not be anxious *or* worried about anything, but in everything [every circumstance and situation] by prayer and petition with thanksgiving, continue to make your [specific] requests known to God. And the peace of God [that peace which reassures the heart, that peace] which transcends all understanding, [that peace which] stands guard over your hearts and your minds in Christ Jesus [is yours]" (Philippians 4:6–7, AMP).

Desperation

I almost lost my mind.
Time and time again, I felt like giving up.
There were even thoughts of suicide.
I didn't want to live; I had had enough.

I can't take another day of hurt and pain.
I'm tired of everything going wrong.
Day in and day out, I fight to survive.
I don't have the strength or courage to move on.

I can't deal with all of the suffering.
I can't cope with all of the agony.
There seems to be battle after battle.
The enemy is always attacking me.

Where oh where can I run?
Where can I find rest for my weary soul?
Who can I turn to
when life has taken its toll?

Where can I find peace?
Please tell me where I can find a little joy.
In the midst of my cry of desperation, I recognize the
sweet voice of Jesus saying,
"You don't have to bear it.
Give it all to me, your Savior and Lord."

CHAPTER 18

EMBRACE IT; DON'T ERASE IT

You're Going to Make It

It happened; you have faced it, and I know you are going to make it. You have stood the test of time. People are amazed at how you have overcome adversity. They are puzzled at how you are still standing after your last storm. They don't understand why you haven't lost your mind after all the hell you endured.

They can't quite put their finger on why you haven't stopped, called it quits, given up, lost hope, or thrown in the towel. They are trying to figure out what you are made of. They can't comprehend how you continue to bounce back time and time again. They can't understand how you keep going with all the opposition you have faced.

People are wondering what makes you tick because they are amazed at how you continue to smile when you should be crying, standing tall when you should have fallen, loving even though you have been hurt, always helping others when you don't have much yourself, and how you find the strength and courage to fight and never give up. They want to know your secret.

They just want to know how you do it. What they fail to understand is that there is no magic potion, no special trick; just a made-up mind. It wasn't simple; it wasn't easy, but you decided to face it. You stopped running; you stopped hiding; you stopped being intimidated by your struggles, trials, and tragedies and decided to face everything that life has thrown your way the good, the bad, and the absolutely ugly.

You have figured out that when you recognize them, face them, and deal with them, somehow life's problems don't appear as big. When we stop trying to erase it and decide to embrace it, then there is no doubt we can make it.

CHAPTER 19

EMBRACE YOUR VALUE

You Are Priceless

Do you know your worth? Do you understand your true value? You are priceless, awesome, an amazing person, and a rare treasure. However, somewhere down along the way, you forgot how precious you really are. Someone started speaking death over your life, telling you that you are worthless, nothing, a nobody; no one wants you, and you will never amount to anything.

Don't listen to the lies of negative people who drain you with their words. Separate yourself from people who don't recognize and can't appreciate your value. Stop listening to the lies of the enemy, as he tries to ambush your mind with reasons why you're not good enough. You are good enough. You are absolutely enough. As a matter of fact, you are more than enough.

Please don't base your self-worth and value only on external factors or what others say or think. Your value is not determined by how you look; where you live, work; education; what you drive; how many friends you have; how many likes you receive on Facebook; or how much money you have saved in the bank. You don't need anyone to validate you in order to prove your worth. A price tag can't be placed on your value. You are priceless. Your value is more precious than jewels, *and* your worth is far above rubies *or* pearls (Proverbs 31:10, AMP). Speak over yourself, encourage yourself, and remind yourself every day that you are worthy and have intrinsic value.

You are invaluable, treasured, cherished, important, unique, priceless, and irreplaceable. Go ahead and embrace your value. Shine bright like a diamond; glitter, glow, and leave a little sparkle wherever you go!

CHAPTER 20

EMBRACE YOUR HATERS

They Really Are Your Encouragers

We ALL have haters! I'm sorry to burst your bubble, but everybody doesn't like you. Everyone is not happy for you. Everybody is not your friend. Everyone is not celebrating your success. There are those who could care less about the awesome things that are happening in your life. You see a lot of people on the sidelines as you stroll down the streets of life.

A lot of people have shown up, but please believe that all of them are not supporters. You have some that are only spectators, watching and waiting for you to fail, to fall, and to lose. They are expecting you to trip, mess up, and give up. They are silent when you are winning, succeeding, and excelling.

However, when all hell has broken loose in your life, they may be smiling and appear to be concerned on the outside, yet, on the inside, they are laughing, dancing, and celebrating your downfall.

You go ahead and live, thrive, excel, succeed, walk in

your purpose, and follow your dreams, but don't forget that the adversary is preying, plotting, and scheming against you. "Satan hath desired to have you, that he may sift you as wheat" (Luke 22:31). "He wants to see you broke, busted, adjusted, losing hope; but I have prayed for thee, that thy faith fail not" (Luke 22:31).

There are people who are not impressed by your certifications, your accolades, the milestones you have reached, or the impact you have made. As a matter of fact, they don't even know you, but they can't stand you. "If the world hates you, know that it hated me before it hated you" (John 15:18). We will have haters, and that's OK.

Go ahead and turn that negative energy from the haters into positive energy by allowing it to fuel you into grinding harder, doing better; show them that in spite of all their hating, in all these things, we are more than conquerors through Him who loved us (Romans 8:37). Don't allow what they do to block or stop you. Don't you dare let your haters make you feel low; rather, let your haters be your elevators. Let them be your motivation. Leave them alone; pay them no attention; give them no thought; don't waste your time or energy dealing with them because if God is for us, who can stand against us? (Romans 8:31). As a matter of fact, sometimes the people that hate you, God will turn around and use those very same people to bless you. Embrace your haters; God will take care of them. "Vengeance is mine, I will repay says the Lord" (Romans 12:19).

LETTER TO MY HATERS

Why are you hating?
Why do you want to play that game?
You are hating on me?
And you don't even know my name.
You see me walking down the street;
you stare me down from head to toe.
You have the audacity to look me dead in my face
without even saying hello!
Why are you tripping?
You don't even know me like that!
Are you hating on me
because when you see me, you see a class act?
You say I am stuck up and conceited
and that I am puffed up with pride.
No, you got it all twisted.
I am a child of the King; that's why I walk with my chest
out, and my head held high!
I am not stuck up, and I'm surely not conceited.
Nor do I think I am better than.
I just know who I am and whose I am,
and I am comfortable in my own skin.
So, go right ahead and hate
if that's the way you chose to be
because all that hating you are doing
is only elevating me!

CHAPTER 21

EMBRACE YOUR BEAUTY

You Are Your Own Kind of Beautiful

You are so absolutely beautiful. You don't need anyone to tell you that you are beautiful. You don't have to try to live up to someone else's definition of beauty. Who decides what beauty is anyway? "Charm *and* grace are deceptive, and [superficial] beauty is vain, But a woman who fears the LORD [reverently worshiping, obeying, serving, and trusting Him with awe-filled respect], she shall be praised" (Proverbs 31:30, AMP). You don't need snap chat filters, Photoshop apps; just the right angle or the perfect lighting to capture how beautiful you are. People look at our outward appearance, but the Lord looks at our heart (1 Samuel 16:7). You are a masterpiece created by the Master. You need no changes, no adjustments, no Botox, no implants, no cosmetic surgeries to make you beautiful because you are fearfully and wonderfully made (Psalms 139:14).

One's outer beauty may capture the eyes, but it will soon fade. However, it's your inner beauty, which is so captivating, intriguing, mesmerizing, that captures the heart. Your inner beauty is what makes you so attractive. You have a beautiful heart and soul that radiates a truly natural beauty that cannot be diluted, overlooked, or ignored.

There is something so appealing, fascinating, graceful, intriguing, enthralling, and elegant about you that make-up can't enhance, a camera can't capture, and even the most stylish clothes can't do it justice because your beauty is just part of your DNA. Your beauty should not come from outward adornments, such as elaborate hairstyles and the wearing of gold jewelry or fine clothes. Rather, it should be that of your inner self, the unfading beauty of a gentle and quiet spirit, which is of great worth in God's sight (1 Peter 3:3–4). Embrace your beauty because you are absolutely positively beautiful from the inside out!

CHAPTER 22

EMBRACE YOUR PLACE

You Belong

You are not a mistake. God knew what He was doing when He created you. It doesn't matter how you got here, where you have been, or what you have done. It was destined for you to be here in this place at this appointed time. You are not here by sheer luck, happenstance, or accident. God has ordained that you be here for such a time as this (Esther 4:14). You were created for a purpose. There is a need in the earth; therefore, God created you to fulfill a specific need. "'For I know the plans I have for you,' declares the LORD, 'plans to prosper you and not to harm you, plans to give you hope and a future'" (Jeremiah 29:11).

You may feel like you are just taking up space. Perhaps you are asking yourself, *Why in the world am I even here? What am I supposed to be doing with my life?* You may think you have nothing to offer no talents, nothing to bring to the table but I beg to differ. I want you to know that you are necessary. You are an asset, valuable, a blessing. Please understand and know that somebody needs you!

They need to hear your voice, see your smiling face, feel your embrace, experience your love, gain knowledge from your wisdom, and receive strength and encouragement from your story.

Someone has found the courage to keep pressing because they saw you persevere. Somebody else has found the energy to tough it out because you didn't give up. You are so busy trying to figure out your significance that you can't see the followers, supporters, admirers, fans that are watching you with their eyes fixed on your every move. They need you! Without you, so many lives just wouldn't be the same. You have so much to offer.

You bring hope, strength, courage, wisdom, love, inspiration, and light. You make things easier, more fun, better, less painful, and more exciting. Never underestimate the value of your presence. The world needs you. So, rise up and embrace your place.

CHAPTER 23

EMBRACE THE WAIT

Timing Is Everything

We live in a society that wants everything right now! We want it quick, in a hurry. We want it when we want it. We want an instantaneous, microwave fast food; next-day delivery type of responses to what's going on in our life. We don't want to wait for anything! We have absolutely no patience. We get mad, frustrated, impatient, angry, and upset when things don't happen when and how we think they should. We give up, are ready to quit, throw a fit, throw in the towel, get mad, get angry, and have pity parties when things don't happen at the snap of our fingers. We want the good times to keep on rolling and the bad times, the hard times, the trouble, struggle, sickness, etc., to be gone in an instant. I hate to be the bearer of bad news, but life doesn't always happen like that. Sometimes you have to wait. So, learn to be patient.

Patience is a virtue. It is a useful skill we can all use. It will save us a lot of frustration and anxiety if we just learn to be patient because waiting is a part of life. We have to wait in line at the grocery store. When you go out to eat on a busy Saturday or Sunday evening, you may have to wait thirty minutes to an hour to be seated. When you go to the DMV at the end or beginning of the month, you may have to take a ticket and wait 1½ hours before your number is called. At the amusement park, you may have to wait in line for a long time to ride your favorite attraction. If you are traveling during a busy holiday, you may find yourself stuck in endless traffic, experiencing layover, delays, or cancellations at the airport or waiting for a train that is behind schedule. There are times we are waiting for a new job, to purchase a home, to buy a car, to launch a business, to recuperate from an illness, and the list goes on. You get the picture; there are times that we just have to wait.

Waiting can be inconvenient and painful, yet sometimes very necessary. Sometimes we want things we are not ready for or can't handle at present. Sometimes we don't want to wait, but waiting is part of the process. A woman finds out that she has conceived and is excited about the bundle of joy growing inside of her, but it's not going to happen overnight. There is a process; there is a waiting period of approximately 9 months, 40 weeks, 280 days as the baby grows and develops inside of the mother. If the baby is born too soon, there is a chance the baby could experience breathing problems, low blood sugar, high-risk health problems, trouble sucking and swallowing, smaller or less developed brain, as well as other complications, and even death. As excited and anxious as a new parent may be, they know there is a wait before they can cuddle their precious child. During the wait, the mother may experience complications such as high blood sugar, swelling, morning sickness, and many other complications. However, she knows that if she is patient, this, too, shall pass because, sometimes, these things happen during the process. She understands that if she focuses on taking care of herself and prepares for the arrival of her child, it will ALL be worth the wait.

As impatient as we are, waiting is not always a bad thing. There are times we desire to have something, and we may not be ready for it yet. There are also times when you are going through a trial or struggle and you wanted it to be over yesterday. However, the very thing you are going through may be what is developing and maturing you for something greater down the road. It could be preparing you for something that you can't even imagine right now, but you want to rush the process. Making you mad, upset, frustrated, and wanting to quit is not what the wait is designed to do. Learn to be patient while you wait. Consider it a sheer gift, friends, when tests and challenges come at you from all sides. You know that under pressure, your faith life is forced into the open and shows its true colors. So, don't try to get out of anything prematurely. Let it do its work so you become mature and well-developed, not deficient in any way (James 1:3–4). Remember that the difficulties of life that we endure didn't come to stay, but they came to pass. Weeping may endure for a night, but joy comes in the morning (Psalm 30:5).

I want to empower you to embrace the wait! I don't care what it looks or feels like. Don't give up; don't stop trying; don't stop pushing; never stop believing. Don't concentrate on the wait; focus on what lies beyond the wait the car, the baby, the house, the degree, the relief, the job, the promotion, the business, the recovery, the financial breakthrough, the healing, the joy. Let us not grow weary *or* become discouraged in doing good, for at the proper time, we will reap if we do not give in (Galatians 6:9).

KEEP HOLDING ON

There is a blessing in your pressing.
There is gain through your pain.
There is a rainbow after the storm clouds.
And there is sunshine after the rain.

There is laughter after your tears.
There is joy after your sorrow.
You may weep all night long,
but thank God those tears will be replaced by a smile on tomorrow.

There is success after your failure.
There is victory after your defeat.
There is a time of great celebration
because you overcame when Satan
thought he had you beat.

There is wholeness after your brokenness.
There is healing after you have been torn apart.
Just a touch from the Master's hand
can heal your wounded spirit and mend your broken
heart.

Keep on pressing on; don't stop.
Giving up is something you cannot afford to do.
Hold on to God's unchanging hand,
for there is a blessing on the other side of through.

CHAPTER 24

EMBRACE FAITH

Faith Will Get You Through

What is faith? Hebrews 11:1 says, "Now faith is the substance of things hoped for, the evidence of things not seen." Anybody, even unbelievers, can have faith when everything is sailing smoothly along. It's easy to say, "Child, you just got to have faith! Believe God, honey!" It is easy to encourage someone else when they are going through, but when trouble comes knocking at your door, it's a different story.

When trouble moves in and unpacks its suitcase at your house, every time you turn around, it's something your money is funny, children not acting right, husband or wife not acting right; you lost your job; cancer invades your body; you experience death in your family; trials, tribulations, and storms are continuously coming at you. Honey, you are going to need more than a big bank account, a good job, a loving husband or wife; you are going to need some faith to see you through!

Faith will keep you. It will keep you together when

everything is falling apart. Faith will give you hope when you feel helpless and things appear hopeless. It is your night vision when you are facing those dark days. Faith is looking beyond what you see now and praising God for what's next. We have got to believe God, no matter what. No matter what our circumstance or situation looks like, no matter what the doctor says, no matter what people say or do, no matter what our bank account looks like, if we exercise our faith, all things are possible. We have to trust

God for what we can't see, what we don't know and understand; that's what faith is.

We must cultivate our faith through prayer, reading the Word, and worship. Through a consistent relationship with our awesome God, we can become strong in our faith. We need to weed out the seeds of fear, doubt, and negativity so that our faith can grow and become strong. When Moses was faced with the Red Sea in front of him, and Pharaoh's army behind him, he didn't have time to sit there and try to figure out whether or not the rod may work. I am sure the people were grumbling and griping behind him, and he didn't have time to pay attention to them. He had to have faith in God, stretch out that rod, and watch God work! When the Lord allows the devil to touch your life like he did Job and take everything you own, it's going to take faith to see you through. Job was just and upright, and look at what happened: His friends come to speculate, and his wife told him to curse God and die. But Job had so much faith and said, "Though he slay me, yet will I trust him" (Job 13:15).

You also know that in order for your faith to increase, you are going to have to be tested. But you can't give up and throw in the towel; you must keep the faith, no matter what comes your way. Don't let go; hold on to your faith. 1 Timothy 4:1 says, "Now the Spirit speaketh expressly, that in the latter times some shall depart from the faith, giving heed to seducing spirits, and doctrines of devils; but don't you dare allow anything or anyone shake your faith in God." As long as you keep trusting, hoping, believing, and having faith in our God, the King of Kings and Lord of Lords, Alpha and Omega, the God of the universe, then no matter how bad a thing is, you will always have the victory!

I encourage you to embrace faith. Just like water is essential to life on earth, so is faith. Faith is our lifeline when we find ourselves overwhelmed by the cares of life. Faith is our life jacket when life throws us overboard into the raging stormy sea of trials and tribulations. Faith is our CPR, our oxygen, our life support when the unexpected shows up and knocks the breath out of our body. My faith is what keeps me, sustains me, gives me hope, and helps me to endure. I believe we can exist without faith, but I don't believe we can truly live and thrive without faith. I know from experience that without faith, I would be so distracted and consumed by what's going on around me, what's happening to me, and what's happening in front of me that I would not be able to see the light at the end of the tunnel. I believe that without faith, I would have no hope. Oh, but with faith, we have hope! We have help from somebody greater, bigger, and wiser than you and I.

With faith, you don't have to rely on your limited thinking and resources, but you can: "Trust in *and* rely confidently on the LORD with all your heart And do not rely on your own insight *or* understanding. [a]In all your ways know *and* acknowledge *and* recognize Him, And He will make your paths straight *and* smooth [removing obstacles that block your way]" (Proverbs 3:5–6).

A Prayer of Faith

Lord, give us an extra measure of faith today. We stand on Your promises, believing in Your Word, knowing that You are able to do exceeding abundantly above all that we ask or think (Ephesians 3:20). We realize that You are our help, our hope, and we trust completely in You.

Lord, renew and deepen our faith in You. Help our lives to be a manifestation of a people who totally rely on You. We want to be steadfast in our faith as we wait on You. We understand that we have limited power, but You have all power. There is nothing too hard for You. Lord, help us to fully rely on You every second of every hour of every day.

When we are encountered with the seen and unforeseen, help us to never forget who You are: "The LORD is my rock, my fortress, and the One who rescues me; My God, my rock *and* strength in whom I trust *and* take refuge; My shield, and the horn of my salvation, my high tower my stronghold" (Psalm 18:2). Help us to be fearless people of faith filled with courage and never doubting. All of our hope is in You. We find great comfort in knowing that You are our Shepherd [to feed, to guide, and to shield me]; we shall not want (Psalm 23:1). We love You, and we thank You. In Jesus' name we pray. Amen.

CHAPTER 25

EMBRACE PRAYER

The Power of Prayer

Prayer is so powerful! I have learned in my 51 years on this earth that every answer to every problem or situation I face can come through prayer. Jesus was matter-of-fact: "Embrace this God-life. Really embrace it, and nothing will be too much for you. This mountain, for instance: Just say, 'Go jump in the lake' no shuffling or shilly-shallying and it's as good as done. That's why I urge you to pray for absolutely everything, ranging from small to large. Include everything as you embrace this God-life, and you'll get God's everything. And when you assume the posture of prayer, remember that it's not all asking.

If you have anything against someone, forgive only then will your heavenly Father be inclined to also wipe your slate clean of sins" (Mark 11:22–25, MSG).

I've come to realize that as brilliant as we, humans, think we are, we have limits. However, prayer connects us to an omnipotent God who has all power, supreme power, and no limitations. He is omniscience, meaning He is all-knowing, and He is omnipresent because He is everywhere at the same time. He can hear all of us, see all of us, know what we are doing, and help all of us at the same time.

You don't need an appointment to talk to Him. You don't have to be perfect or have a degree because there is no respect of persons with God (Romans 2:11). His line is never busy at any time. His calls don't drop, and you always have service when you call Him. This is why I pray. I need to talk to somebody who doesn't judge, who doesn't compare; someone who hears me in spite of my flaws, who won't walk away, and who won't gossip about me to everybody else. "The LORD *is* near to all who call upon Him" (Psalm 145:18).

We need to set aside time every day to pray. It needs to become a part of our lifestyle. We need to develop a culture of prayer. "Be persistent *and* devoted to prayer, being alert *and* focused in your prayer life with *an attitude of* thanksgiving" (Colossians 4:2). "Then He spoke a parable to them, that men always ought to pray and not lose heart" (Luke 18:1). Prayer will help you endure, help you stand, give you strength, keep you pressing, and give you hope. "Constantly rejoicing in hope [because of our confidence in Christ], steadfast and patient in distress, devoted to prayer [continually seeking wisdom, guidance, and strength]" (Romans 12:12, AMP).

Prayer is for everybody every day. It does not matter how spectacular or how grueling your day is, we should take time to pray. When I was dealing with domestic violence and then divorce, prayer kept me sane. Prayer kept me going at times when I wanted to just quit. When I did not know what to do, God gave me direction through prayer. I was comforted through prayer. "Do not be anxious *or* worried about anything, but in everything [every circumstance and situation] by prayer and petition with thanksgiving, continue to make your [specific] requests known to God. [7] And the peace of God [that peace which reassures the heart, that peace] which transcends all understanding, [that peace which] stands guard over your hearts and your minds in Christ Jesus [is yours]" (Philippians 4:6–7, AMP). It does not matter what you encounter in life, a consistent prayer life partnered with faith can see you through it all. "Rejoice always *and* delight in your faith; [17] be unceasing *and* persistent in prayer; [18] in every situation [no matter what the circumstances] be thankful *and* continually give thanks *to God*; for this is the will of God for you in Christ Jesus" (1 Thessalonians 5:16–18, AMP).

God wants to talk to you. He is waiting and ready to listen. You don't have to speak eloquently or pray this long-drawn-out prayer. Speak from your heart. Call His name. Don't be afraid. Just talk to Him as if you are talking to a friend or family member. You don't need a special occasion or a tragedy to happen to pray. Thank Him for what He has done. Praise Him for who He is! Ask Him to help you, heal you, or forgive you. Pray and believe and watch God move and work in your life like never before. Prayer partnered with faith is super powerful.

"For this reason I am telling you, whatever things you ask for in prayer [in accordance with God's will], believe [with confident trust] that you have received them, and they will be *given* to you" (Mark 11:24). "And whatever you ask for in prayer, believing, you will receive" (Matthew 21:22).

I do want you to understand this about prayer: Prayer is not magic, but it works, and God moves in supernatural ways, which is by far greater than any magic I have ever seen. Prayer does not mean everything will work out the way you want, but God will work things out according to His plan. Prayer does not mean you won't have problems, but I promise you, from my personal experience, that prayer will hold you together when you are falling apart.

Having a prayer life will give you peace in the midst of chaos. I need you to promise me that you will embrace prayer. It will change your life like nothing else ever has, can, or will. "Make this your common practice: Confess your sins to each other and pray for each other so that you can live together whole and healed. The prayer of a person living right with God is something powerful to be reckoned with" (James 5:16).

PRAYER

When life is beautiful, and everything is
going according to plan, I pray.
When life is spiraling out of control, and it seems
as if trouble is on every hand, I pray.
When I am enjoying success and feeling
happy and blessed, I pray.
When I am going through, and everything
appears to be a mess, I pray.
When I am surrounded by acquaintances,
family, and friends, I pray.
When I can't find anyone to lean or depend on, I pray.
When the sun is shining, and there are no
clouds in the sky, I pray.
When the storms of life are raging and
tossing me from side to side, I pray.
When the road is smooth, and I can clearly see my way,
I pray.

When I am standing at the crossroads of life and don't
know which path to take, I pray.
Early in the morning, I pray.
All through the day, as I travel along the way, I pray.
In the evening, before I go to bed, I pray.
In the midnight hour, when I can't sleep because I have
a million things going through my head, I pray.
Men should always pray and not faint.
I tried living life without prayer, but I couldn't.
The effectual fervent prayer of the
righteous availeth much.

Prayer is a powerful weapon that is available to all of us.

Prayer is our line of communication.
Prayer is where God speaks to us and gives us
revelation.
God desires to talk to us through prayer.
When we kneel to pray, He will meet us there.
Prayer is where I find peace, relief, connection, direction,
clarification, confirmation, revelation, strength,
power, help, and hope.

Apart from prayer, I am weak, weary, confused,
wayward, helpless, hopeless, and I just can't cope.
Prayer is my secret place,
my happy place
where I bask in His presence
and seek the Master's face.
Prayer is a special time where I go to my Father,
and He meets me there.

It's a place where I praise Him and thank Him and
where I can also leave every burden, worry, and care.
Prayer is what gives us hope, joy, and helps us survive in
the times in which we live.
In order to stand, we must learn how to kneel.
I'll say it to you; you and people everywhere
if you desire to live an abundant life,
develop a culture of prayer!

CHAPTER 26

EMBRACE FORGIVENESS

You Have Been Exonerated

Bitter, angry, and seething with unforgiveness that's how some of us are living our lives. We are stuck, bound, unable to love as we should, battling in our relationships and within ourselves because of the hate, resentment, bad blood, and deep-seated animosity we have allowed to infest our hearts and minds. This is exactly what the enemy wanted. He wants you to be so consumed with the bad deed, the offense, the person that did you wrong, the people that hurt you, how you hurt others or yourself that you can't even begin to think about forgiving them.

He doesn't want us to forgive ourselves for the wrong we have done. Some of us have been bound by unforgiveness for days, months, years, and decades. I know of people who have, unfortunately, went to their grave holding onto unforgiveness. The enemy wants to see you miserable, filled with resentment, reminding you over and over again, opening the wound of that bad situation, that thing, that person, that pain that has you restrained through unforgiveness. He doesn't want you to do this: "Love your enemies and pray for those who persecute you, so that you may be sons of your Father who is in heaven" (Matthew 5:44–45).

I understand that you have been hurt. I know that it is painful. I can imagine what it feels like when you have been offended, lied on, misused, abused, slandered, defamed, ashamed, almost driven insane, nearly lost your life because of something someone said or did or even something you inflicted upon yourself. I am well aware that it's not always easy to forgive, but do it anyway. There is freedom in forgiveness. When you forgive, it relieves you, releases you, and lifts the burden off your heart and mind. Don't give the devil anymore opportunity to cripple you with unforgiveness. He would love for you to remain bitter, angry, and remorseful.

He desires to see you hand-cuffed to unforgiveness so he can zap your power, water down your praise, and pull the plug on your prayer life. I encourage you to let all bitterness, wrath, anger, clamor, and slander be put away from you, along with all malice. "Be kind to one another, tender-hearted, forgiving each other, just as God in Christ also has forgiven you" (Ephesians 4:31–32). Remember that forgiveness is just as much for you as it is the other person.

Live, love, forgive, and forget. You can't change the past. What has happened has happened. What has been said has been said. What has been done has been done. Nothing you do now can change what has been, but your future will be so much happier when you divorce unforgiveness. Let go of the bitterness, anger, resentment, hate, remorse that you have held onto for far too long. Learn to forgive quickly, and you will receive untold peace and experience the happiness that true freedom brings. My prayer is that God will free you from the stronghold of offense and unforgiveness.

We will no longer allow the enemy to cause us to harbor unforgiveness in our hearts and minds. We will not entertain unforgiveness and allow it to draw a wedge between our relationships with others or with God. The enemy wants us to be sentenced to a life of unforgiveness. Jesus wants you to be free! He endured the cross so that we can be free. The enemy has NO power. Jesus has ALL power, which means He has the power to heal us, forgive us, and help us to genuinely forgive others. Let us embrace forgiveness so we can love freely, speak compassionately, laugh heartily, forgive quickly and live passionately, fully, and well.

CHAPTER 27

EMBRACE JOY

Developing an Attitude of Gratitude

Life is much too short for us to spend our days being mad, angry, bitter, sour, and upset over things that most of the time we can't change. I would hate to live my days in anxiety, depressed, frustrated, and crying all the time. We may be able to justify why we should feel these emotions; however, I choose joy because the joy of the Lord is my strength (Nehemiah 8:10).

I am sure we can find plenty to complain about, but why? We must not allow our circumstances, what's going on around us, and the negative/toxic people who may be around us to dictate how we feel. We must not allow anything or anyone to have that much power over us. However, we must develop an attitude of gratitude and just be thankful and learn to find the good in every situation. I've learned by now to be quite content, whatever my circumstances. I'm just as happy with little as with much, with much as with little. I've found the recipe for being happy, whether full or hungry, hands full or hands empty. Whatever I have, wherever I am, I can make it through anything in the One who makes me who I am (Philippians 4:11–13).

The sorrows, cares, and storms of life will try to zap your joy, peace, and happiness. Ask me, "How?" I know because things, people, circumstances, life tried to rob me of my joy. I fell prey to it for a moment. I had my pity party and wallowed in my pain and sorrows for a minute. Then I realized this was no way for me to live and not the way God intended for me to live. God turned things around for me. "You have turned my mourning into dancing for me; You have taken off my sackcloth and clothed me with joy, ^{12} That my soul may sing praise to You and not be silent. O LORD my God, I will give thanks to You forever" (Psalm 30:11–12, AMP). I made a decision to be joyful in spite of, in the middle of, regardless of, no matter what, who, when, why, or where; I shall be joyful. "Though the fig tree does not blossom, And there is no fruit on the vines.

Though the yield of the olive fails, And the fields produce no food, Though the flock is cut off from the fold, And there are no cattle in the stalls, ^{18} Yet I will [choose to] rejoice in the LORD; I will [choose to] shout in exultation in the [victorious] God of my salvation!" (Habakkuk 3:17–18).

My prayer for you is that you will live a life full of peace, love, contentment, and lots of happiness. You will have days you are not totally feeling the joy thing, but don't stay there. "Remember that All you saints! Sing your hearts out to GOD! Thank him to his face! He gets angry once in a while, but across a lifetime there is only love. The nights of crying your eyes out give way to days of laughter(joy)" (Psalm 30:5, MSG). "My friends, embrace joy! And now, GOD, do it again bring rains to our drought-stricken lives. So those who planted their crops in despair will shout hurrahs at the harvest, So those who went off with heavy heart will come home laughing, with armloads of blessing" (Psalm 126:5–6, MSG).

I STILL HAVE JOY

I have been lied on, talked about.
Lord knows I have been mistreated.
Yet, I still have joy.
My body has been invaded by cancer.
I am losing my hair and my appetite
and sometimes left with little energy.
Yet, I still have joy.
I have been laid off from my job,
had to let the bank take my car,
can barely make ends meet.
Yet, I still have joy.
My best friend turned their back on me;
they walked out when I needed them the most.
Yet, I still have joy.
I am a single parent.
The struggle is real when you are doing it all by yourself.
Yet, I still have joy.
I lost my child to gun violence.
You talking about tough;

I thought I was going to absolutely lose my mind.
Yet, I still have joy.
I have a child in jail.
No money for a lawyer or bail.
I hate seeing him locked behind those bars.
Yet, I still have joy.
My body has been attacked by sickness and disease.
I can't get around like I used to.
It's hard.
Yet, I still have joy.

It seems like there are trials and trouble on every hand.
Before you can get out of one storm, here comes
another.
It seems like trouble never takes a break.
Yet, I still have joy.
Mother gone, and father too.
A lot of my friends and family have left this world.
I know I don't have long.
Yet, I still have joy.
We can have joy in the midst of everything we are
confronted with in life.
We know that such joy can only come from knowing
and living for Jesus Christ.

CHAPTER 28

EMBRACE LIFE

Live!

Life is far too short to spend it worrying, angry, and depressed. "Whereas ye know not what shall be on the morrow. For what is your life? It is even a vapour, that appeareth for a little time, and then vanishes away" (James 4:14). We should not spend our time on earth regretting yesterday and dreading tomorrow. We should be intentional, living life to the fullest and maximizing every single moment. Yesterday is gone, and tomorrow is not promised.

Deal with the problems that are facing you today. Don't burden yourself with the problems of days past or overwhelm yourself worrying about what lies ahead. "Therefore, do not be anxious, saying, 'What shall we eat?' or 'What shall we drink?' or 'What shall we wear?' For the Gentiles seek after all these things, and your heavenly Father knows that you need them all. But seek first the kingdom of God and his righteousness, and all these things will be added to you. Therefore do not be anxious about tomorrow, for tomorrow will be anxious for itself. Sufficient for the day is its own trouble" (Matthew 6:31–34). Enjoy this moment. Seize today!

Learn to live and love the life God gave you. Don't compare your life to or try to measure up to someone else because you will always feel inferior. Stay in your lane and walk the path God has paved out for you. "Trust in *and* rely confidently on the LORD with all your heart. And do not rely on your own insight *or* understanding. In all your ways know *and* acknowledge *and* recognize Him, And He will make your paths straight *and* smooth [removing obstacles that block your way]" (Proverbs 3:5–6, AMP). When we allow God to be our tour guide through the journey of life and willingly follow His lead, our difficulties will become clearer, and our burdens lighter.

Starting today, we are going to stop agonizing over what could have, should have, or would have. If we can't change it, we are going to let it go and move on. We will no longer allow ourselves to be consumed with hate, bitterness, resentment, regret, unforgiveness, and all those things that prevent us from living life to the full. We will not waste another moment sitting around, having pity parties. We are not entertaining any whining or complaining.

We are reprogramming our thinking. I believe that if we change our mindset and look for the positive in every situation, we will start to see life a whole lot differently. Stop giving your problems and circumstances so much power by focusing on them all the time. Think about the good, the positive things in life. Summing it all up, friends, I'd say you'll do best by filling your minds and meditating on things true, noble, reputable, authentic, compelling, gracious the best, not the worst; the beautiful, not the ugly; things to praise, not things to curse (Philippians 4:8, AMP).

We need to watch what we think, but we should also be careful as to how to speak to and about ourselves. Words kill; words give life; they're either poison or fruit you choose (Proverbs 18:21, MSG). So, start encouraging yourself. Speak life over every situation. Speak life over every dead situation. Speak victory over difficult situations. Speak that you are the head and not the tail. You are above and not beneath. You are the lender and not the borrower. Speak that your finances are improving, your body is being healed; your mind is at peace; your children are doing well; things are coming together. Just open your mouth and speak! Speak healing, deliverance, salvation, and restoration. We name it, claim it, and speak that we are whole, complete, living, loving, and thriving.

Your life will never be perfect, but it can be productive, promising, and purposeful. Remember, we are going to have trials, test, frustrations, struggles, obstacles, setbacks, and opposition, but we cannot stop. We must never stop believing, hoping, trusting, dreaming, pressing, pursuing, anticipating, expecting, and praying. With God on our side, we can fully embrace each and every moment, regardless of the situation. So, what do you think? With God on our side like this, how can we lose?

If God didn't hesitate to put everything on the line for us, embracing our condition and exposing Himself to the worst by sending His own Son, is there anything else He wouldn't gladly and freely do for us? And who would dare tangle with God by messing with one of God's chosen? Who would dare even to point a finger? The One who died for us who was raised to life for us is in the presence of God at this very moment, sticking up for us. Do you think anyone is going to be able to drive a wedge between us and Christ's love for us? There is no way! Not trouble, not hard times, not hatred, not hunger, not homelessness, not bullying threats, not backstabbing, not even the worst sins listed in the Scripture.

None of this fazes us because Jesus loves us. I'm absolutely convinced that nothing nothing living or dead, angelic or demonic, today or tomorrow, high or low, thinkable or unthinkable absolutely *nothing* can get between us and God's love because of the way that Jesus, our Master, has embraced us. We don't have to be overwhelmed by life. Jesus embraced us; therefore, we can embrace life and LIVE!

CHAPTER 29

EMBRACE IT

It Was Necessary

It is good for me that I was afflicted (Psalms 119:71). It was necessary. It's part of our story. We had to go through that to get to this. We had to suffer over there in order to celebrate the victory over here. We had to cry over there so that we could rejoice over here. We had to go through the storm so that we could view the beautiful rainbow and see the bright golden sun shine down over us after the drenching storm. We had to be broken then so we would have strength for what's coming. Our suffering is necessary. It did not come to break or kill us, but it came to build us, propel us, and to prepare us to walk in our purpose and fulfill our destiny.

Don't hate, regret, despise, or resent all the pain you have endured in your life. What you consider as a curse in your life, God is using to bless someone else's life. That thing that hurt you, you are using to heal someone else. What almost killed you, you are now using to speak life to someone else. What almost made you lose your mind, you are now using to speak peace to someone else. What made you almost lose all hope, you are now using to give hope to someone else. What made you fall, you are now using to help someone else stand. What made you almost give up, you are now using to give someone else the courage to keep pressing on.

What made you almost give up on God, you are now using to help someone else draw closer to God. That thing that ripped you apart, you are using to help someone else hold it together. You see, your tears have not been wasted, and your pain has a purpose. Therefore, my beloved brothers and sisters, be steadfast, immovable, always excelling in the work of the Lord [always doing your best and doing more than is needed], being *continually* aware that your labor [even to the point of exhaustion] in the Lord is not futile *nor* wasted [it is never without purpose]. It hurt you, but because of it, you were able to share, help, and minister to someone else. You see, it wasn't in vain at all. It was necessary; therefore, face it. Embrace it and LIVE!

ACKNOWLEDGMENTS

First and foremost, I want to thank God for the gifts, talents, and abilities that He has given me. I thank God for choosing me to share the empowerment nuggets contained in the pages of this book with the world for such a time as this. I must take this opportunity to show some love and gratitude to those who have had my back, held it down, prayed for me, encouraged me, pushed me, and believed in me when I didn't believe in myself.

I would like to give a big shout-out to my husband who is always there to listen, give advice, and support me, no questions asked. I want to give a shout-out to my girls Endia, Jamyrah, and Chelsea who are always on the sidelines, cheering me on until I cross the finish line.

I can't begin to express my appreciation for my parents Joseph and Lucy Hall, Patricia Atkins, James and Judy Gregory for always being there as a sounding board, to love, to sow into whatever project I'm working on, and to tell me how proud they are of me. I have nothing but love for my sisters and brothers: Patricia, Joyce, Joseph, Phyllis, Nisie, Leon, and Andre. I know they believe in me, and I know they always have my back!

To my mentor Nicole Bonds, who helped me take my confidence to an entirely new level and showed me things about myself that I had overlooked or underestimated, which she saw as greatness. To my mentor Vanessa Canteberry, who was a complete stranger that I met on Facebook but took me under her wings and poured into me, pulled things out of me, pushed me, and encouraged me until I took the final leap and started writing.

There are other family members and friends who have impacted my life, encouraged me, and believed in me until I finally stepped over fear and procrastination, stepped out, stepped up to the plate, and now finally birthing my first book. I am ecstatic, excited, humbled, and grateful about the season that I am in and for the awesome tribe that God has blessed me with.

ABOUT THE AUTHOR

Energetic, inspiring, empowering and captivating are just a few of the adjectives used to describe the multi-talented, Yvette Urquhart. Yvette enjoys every opportunity she is given to use her talents to be a blessing to others. She is an empowerment speaker extraordinaire, clean comedienne, poet, writer, actress and now author.

Yvette travels all over the state of Virginia, North Carolina and beyond using her God given abilities to empower, bring laughter, love, joy, hope and inspiration wherever she goes. As much as she loves inspiring others and entertaining, nothing is more rewarding or gives her as much satisfaction as being the mother of three beautiful daughters; Endia, Jamyrah and Chelsea and a wife to James Urquhart.

Yvette enjoyed a career with Nationwide Insurance Company for 23 years; however, with the genuine love and passion that she has for people, she knew that there was an even greater purpose and plan that God has for her life. It took a couple of years of hesitation and fear before she decided to take a leap of faith and pursue her childhood dream of becoming an empowerment speaker and successful entertainer in which she would stir up the gifts that God has given her and use them to bless men, women, boys and girls everywhere!

Yvette has a way of capturing the attention of the audience whether she is delivering an empowering message as a keynote speaker or arresting their attention while performing an original poetry piece. Yvette is a published poet and also received the honor of distinguished poet from the National Library of Poetry. As a clean comedienne, Yvette is the creator of her inspirational, sensational and hilariously funny alter ego, Hassie Mae Collins Smith Higginbotham Brown, affectionately known as "Ms. Hassie Mae."

Yvette feels right at home on stage as she has written several plays and has also enjoyed being part of the cast of several local plays. One of her plays, "Journey of Faith from the Slave House to the White House," aired on our local station, Channel CW5 and the hit stage play, "Mama's Pearls," landed her on stage at the Black Theatre Festival in Washington, DC.

Yvette resides in Long Island, VA where she is immensely involved in her community and seeks out every opportunity to serve and use her God given abilities to bless and be a blessing. She is a member of the Minority Council for Gretna Middle School. Yvette is a member of the board for the Bridge Community Center in Gretna, VA where she also helps tutor students in their after school program. She is also a volunteer/group leader at the local domestic violence shelter, Frannie's House, where she inspires, encourages, trains, empowers and provides emotional support to victims and survivors of domestic violence. She is a junior at Liberty University where she is pursuing a Bachelor's in Communication.

She is employed part-time through Liberty's school of Osteopathic Medicine. Yvette enjoys making individuals feel their own kind of beautiful as a Mary Kay Independent Beauty Consultant. Yvette is extremely active in her church where she serves as a table leader in the Women's ministry, storyteller in the children's ministry and volunteers during Vacation Bible School. Yvette is founder of Stir Up the Gift Ministry and co-founder of Sisters of Strength International Women's Ministry. Yvette has a sincere heart and love for children of all ages and works with Pastor Kell & First Lady Paulette Stone of Gospel Tabernacle Outreach Center in Gretna, VA as the coordinator of their youth ministry; Kingdom Kids, a church for kids in grades K-12.

Yvette is very humbled for the gifts she has been given and is convinced that her assignment and purpose is to share them with everyone she is fortunate enough to come in contact with along life's journey. Yvette is a lover of life and believes in unleashing the best her everyday. She is dedicated to living life to the fullest so that she can die empty having given every part of herself to loving, helping, empowering, impacting and serving others. If she can do this, then she believes she will have fulfilled God's divine plan for her life.

Feel free to stay connected with Yvette Urquhart on Social Media at:

www.Facebook.com/EmbraceLifeWithYvette
www.Instgram.com/EmbraceLifeWithYvette
www.Twitter.com/letsembracelife
www.Youtube.com/EmbraceLifeWithYvette
www.EmbraceLifeWithYvette.com

www.ingramcontent.com/pod-product-compliance
Lightning Source LLC
Chambersburg PA
CBHW071617040426
42452CB00009B/1376